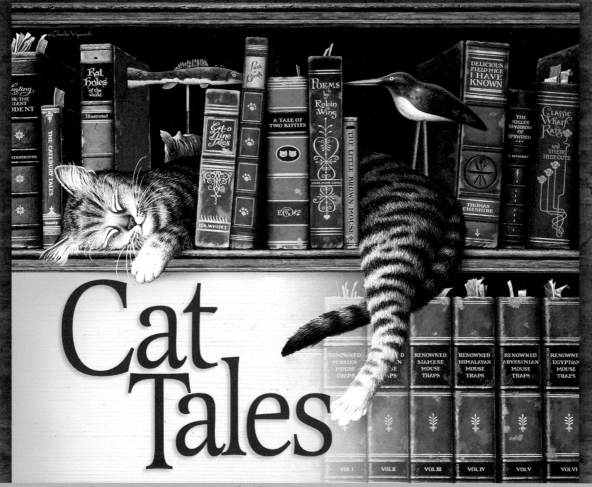

Cat Tales

Snippets on Life from Our Favorite Felines

TEXT AND PAINTINGS BY

Charles Wysocki

HARVEST HOUSE PUBLISHERS
EUGENE, OREGON

Cat Tales

Text Copyright © 2002 by Harvest House Publishers
Published by Harvest House Publishers
Eugene, Oregon 97402

Wysocki, Charles.
   Cat tales / Charles Wysocki.
        p. cm.
   ISBN 0-7369-1024-7 (alk. paper)
   1. Wysocki, Charles—Themes, motives. 2. Cats in art. 3. Cats—Anecdotes. I. Title.
   ND237.w97 A4 2002
   759.13—dc21

                                                                    2002004993

Design and production by Garborg Design Works, Minneapolis, Minnesota

Harvest House Publishers has made every effort to trace the ownership of all poems and quotes. In the event of a question arising from the use of a poem or quote, we regret any error made and will be pleased to make the necessary correction in future editions of this book.

Printed in Hong Kong

03 04 05 06 07 08 09 10 11 / NG / 10 9 8 7 6 5

I love cats because I enjoy my home; and little by little, they become its visible soul.

JEAN COCTEAU

The Wysocki family has always enjoyed having cats. Over the years, I've tried to capture each of their distinct personalities on canvas. My wife, Liz, and I take great pleasure in naming each painting and researching all the little details that go with them. It's my pleasure to share with you the stories behind these favored felines.

And although no one ever truly "owns" a cat, every one of these colorful characters has made our lives richer with each purr, nuzzle, lick, nudge, and nap.

Enjoy!

Charles Wysocki ♡

Did you ever hear of a thing like that?
Oh, what a proud mysterious cat.

VACHEL LINDSAY

A Prickly Pair and Poncho

Of all God's creatures there is only one that cannot be made the slave of the lash. That one is the cat. If man could be crossed with a cat it would improve man, but it would deteriorate the cat.

MARK TWAIN

Our garden-crazy cat, Poncho, posed for this painting. He loves to roll in the sand and he's also become aware of how cactus plants can be "unfriendly" if you get too close. I put him in this precarious position to add a note of levity and mild danger. The cactus wrens are a tease to a sleeping Poncho who, in his dreams, may have other plans for the birds.

Come, lovely cat, and rest upon my heart,
And let my gaze dive in the cold
Live pools of thine enchanted eyes that dart
Metallic rays of green and gold.

CHARLES BAUDELAIR

Cats are beautiful and graceful animals, soft and sleek to the touch, amicable in expression, patient with children who carry them about with hind legs dangling, amusing when they pounce upon a ball of crinkled cellophane or chase the spots of dappled sunlight on a wall. Cats are small and clean and cuddlesome.

MURIEL BEADLE
The Cat

Cats are a mysterious kind of folk. There is

To err is human, to purr is feline.

ROBERT BYRNE

When the tea is brought at five o'clock,
And all the neat curtains are drawn with care,
The little black cat with bright green eyes
Is suddenly purring there.

At first she pretends, having nothing to do,
She has come in merely to blink by the grate.
But, though tea may be late and the milk may be sour,
She is never late.

HAROLD MONRO

The cats particularly. They seem to know. You can fool everybody, but landy M deary-me, you can't fool a cat. They seem to know who's not right, if you know what I mean.

DEWITT BODEEN

more passing in their minds than we are aware of.

SIR WALTER SCOTT

7

Cats sleep anywhere, any table, any chair.
Top of piano, window-ledge, in the middle, on the edge.
Open drawer, empty shoe, anybody's lap will do.
Fitted in a cardboard box, in the cupboard with your frocks.
Anywhere! They don't care! Cats sleep anywhere.

ELEANOR FARJEON

All Burned Out

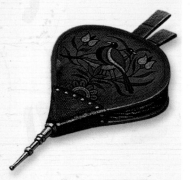

What greater gift than the love of a cat?

CHARLES DICKENS

Max and Remington have always been pals and I wanted to display their special affection in the position they have most frequently fallen into. Their magnet-like attraction naturally called for a setting just as warm as their attachment. What better than a snooze in the glow of the fireplace? This loving couple is a constant joy to watch because I never know what to expect with them and their sleeping gymnastic style. The little fellers in the background are enjoying some confident, playful moments in the land of these sleeping giants.

Dudley Wadsworth Catsinbag

Dudley can always be relied on to think he has again found the ideal hideaway. He seems to enjoy a certain experienced attitude as the cavalier explorer at large. Oblivious to danger, he seeks out alien territory, crawling confidently into things, spaces, and underbrush. Most cats are naturally curious but Dudley has developed his skills beyond the norm of other felines. He may be gone for many hours, even days, from the room and board of his keepers, testing and defying the dangers of some of nature's more aggressive creatures. To this day, but true to his nature, he has returned victorious after a long contented day of staking out his now secret territories and hiding places. Not all cats just "eat" and "sleep." There are the Dudley Wadsworth Catsinbags out there to keep reminding us of that.

We cannot, without becoming cats,
perfectly understand the cat mind.

St. George Mivart

By associating with the cat one only

Most people think that the cat is an unintelligent animal, fond of ease, and caring little for anything but mice and milk. But a cat has really more character than most human beings, and gets a great deal more satisfaction out of life. Of all the animal kingdom, the cat has the most many-sided character.

He—or she—is an athlete, a musician, an acrobat, a Lothario, a grim fighter, a sport of the first water. All day long the cat loafs about the house, takes things easy, sleeps by the fire, and allows himself to be pestered by the attentions of our women-folk and annoyed by our children. To pass the time away he sometimes watches a mouse hole for an hour or two—just to keep himself from dying of ennui; and people get the idea that this sort of thing is all that life holds for the cat. But watch him as the shades of evening fall, and you see the cat as he really is.

Andrew Barton Paterson
The Cat

risks becoming richer.

COLETTE

Cats make exquisite
photographs. They don't keep
bouncing at you to be kissed just
as you get the lens adjusted.

GLADYS TABER

O little cat with yellow eyes,
Enthroned upon my garden gate,
Remote, impassive and sedate
And so unutterably wise.

HELEN VAUGAN WILLIAMS

The cat went here and there
And the moon spun round like a top,
And the nearest kin of the moon,
The creeping cat, looked up.

Black Minnaloushe stared at the moon,
For, wander and wail as he would,
The pure cold light in the sky,
Troubled his animal blood...

Does Minnaloushe know that his pupils
Will pass from change to change,
And that from round to crescent,
From crescent to round they range?

Minnaloushe creeps through the grass
Alone, important and wise,
And lifts to the changing moon
His changing eyes.

W. B. YEATS

Cats are designated friends.

NORMAN CORWIN

13

Cats are a tonic, they are a laugh, they are a cuddle, they are at least pretty just about all of the time and beautiful some of the time.

ROGER CARAS

Elmer and Loretta

In my house lives a cat who is a curmudgeon and cantankerous, a cat who is charming and convivial, and a cat who is combative and commendable. And yet I have but one cat.

DAVE EDWARDS

This painting is my sincere tribute to all of the wonderful dedicated pharmacists whose skills help keep us in good health. My original concept was of a squeaky clean environment. Then, thinking back to my childhood and my mom's potions foisted on me when I was ailing set my thoughts in this daring direction. It turned out to be an exciting excursion using fictionalized worldwide medications all done, of course, with tongue in cheek. My interest grew thicker when I delved into researching old remedy books and catalogs. Then I began to improvise to the point of ridiculousness. I look back now and realize how terribly dull "clean and squeaky" would have been. If I have offended certain members or all of the society of drug practitioners, I'm sorry that you are not dancing to the same music of my dizzy world. Seems as though Elmer and Loretta are more than content in this somewhat cluttered atmosphere.

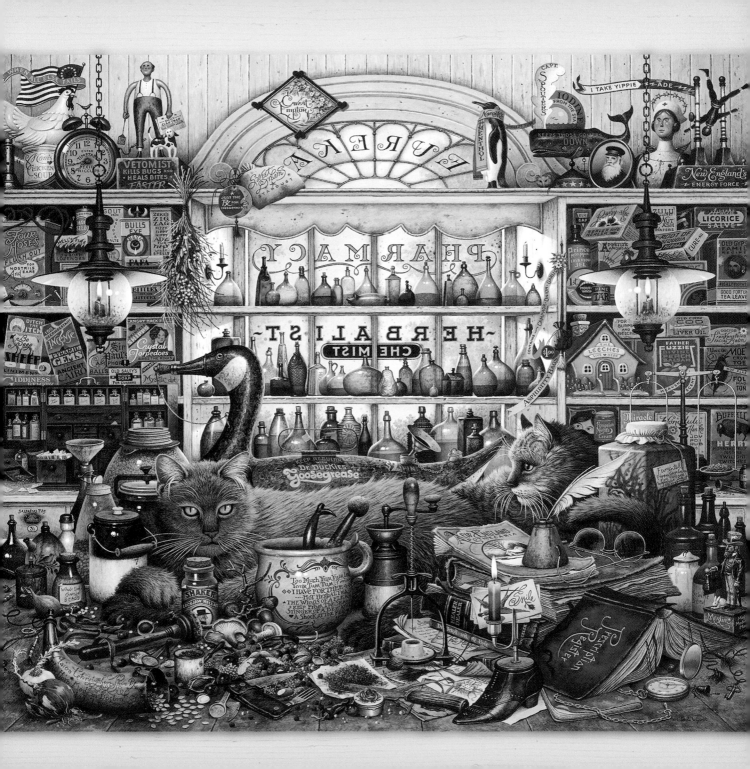

> *A home without a cat—and a well-fed,*
> *well-petted and properly revered cat—may be a*
> *home, perhaps, but how can it prove title?*
>
> MARK TWAIN

Ethel the Gourmet

Ethel was baptized "Ethel" in honor of the neighbor friend of the Ricardos on the *I Love Lucy* television show, Ethel Mertz. She liked to hang out in the kitchen and although the other cats would eat and run, she stuck around and became "Ethel the Gourmet." Ethel, with that licking, winning smile, was a difficult drawing exercise. I can't begin to tell you how many tongues, mouth caverns, and teeth I plowed through to get to what I finally came up with. The fun of working with cat-related food items proved to be quite a research project at the supermarket and specialty gourmet shops. Liz and I laughed ourselves silly with the label messages. This painting took me a long time to organize, illustrate, design, and letter with all of the labels needing that special attention.

From his admirers he evokes an intense adoration which usually finds an outlet in exaggerated expression. It is practically impossible for a cat-lover to meet a stray feline on the street without stopping to pass the time of day with him.

CARL VAN VECHTEN
The Tiger in the House

As legend describes, a cat may live at least nine lives, but kittens are carried by angels.

LUCINDA A. LILAMOORE

Hear our prayer, Lord, for all animals.
May they be well-fed and well-trained and happy;
Protect them from hunger and fear and suffering;
And, we pray, protect especially, dear Lord,
The little cat who is the companion of our home,
Keep her safe as she goes abroad,
And bring her back to comfort us.

AUTHOR UNKNOWN

...the playful kitten, with its pretty little tigerish gambols, is infinitely more amusing than half the people one is obliged to live with in the world.

LADY MORGAN

No matter how much cats fight, there

It is my conviction that cats never forget anything...a cat's brain is much less cluttered with extraneous matters than a human's.

PAUL COREY

18

If there was any petting to be done...he chose to do it. Often he would sit looking at me, and then, moved by a delicate affection, come and pull at my coat and sleeve until he could touch my face with his nose, and then go away contented.

CHARLES DUDLEY WARNER

always seem to be plenty of kittens.

ABRAHAM LINCOLN

I think I could turn and live with animals,
they are so placid and self-contained,
I stand and look at them long and long.

WALT WHITMAN

19

Frederick the Literate

This painting was a memorial to Frederick the cat, who was killed by a car in 1991. Fred was always sleeping on a bookshelf so we wanted to remember him like that. When I was putting the painting together, I decided that the titles of the books on the shelves should all have something to do with cats. Liz and I sat through breakfasts, lunches, and dinners trying to come up with titles. We even traveled with a pad and pen so we could write down any titles we thought of.

This painting was most difficult to work on, not only because of my emotional attachment to dear Frederick but also because of the many hours spent designing the lettering style on the book spines. I really enjoyed the tedium because it proved that discipline has its rewards. In the cat series, Frederick seems to be "the" favorite.

A cat pours his body on the floor like water.
It is restful just to see him.

WILLIAM LYON PHELPS

Herkymer

Herkymer, in this primitive-mode style of painting, depicts an exhausted cat who never exudes any more energy other than his trips to the feeding pan. So this unusually active "cat-and-mouse game" had to be put on canvas to verify that Herkymer does have some stored energy that surfaces, but only when he desires.

Two things are aesthetically perfect in the world—the clock and the cat.

EMILE AUGUSTE CHARTIER

The really great thing about cats is their endless variety. One can pick a cat to fit almost any kind of decor, color, scheme, income, personality, or mood. But under the fur, whatever color it may be, there still lies, essentially unchanged, one of the world's free souls.

ERIC GURNEY

There's no need for a piece of sculpture in a

Agreeable friends—
they ask no questions,
they pass no criticisms.

GEORGE ELLIOT

There is a feud between the cat and
the dog, but this dislike is superficial
and can, in most instances, be easily
set aside. It is, to be sure, instinctive.
Kittens with their eyes scarcely open
have been known to spit at a dog.
But cats who live with dogs usually
do so with dignity and ease;
in many cases a deep affection
springs up between the two.

CARL VAN VECHTEN
The Tiger in the House

We can judge the heart of a man by his treatment of animals.

IMMANUEL KANT

home that has a cat.

WESLEY BATES

Marco turned and stood with his back against the door. The cat had awakened and she was gazing at him with her green eyes. She began to purr encouragingly. She really helped Marco to think. He was thinking with all his might and trying to remember...

The cat miauled again, this time very anxiously indeed. The kittens heard her and began to squirm and squeak piteously.

"Lead me to this little thing," said Marco, as if speaking to Something in the darkness about him, and he got up.

He put his hand out toward the kittens, and it touched something lying not far from them. It must have been lying near his elbow all night while he slept.

It was the key! It had fallen upon the shelf, and not on the floor at all.

Marco picked it up and then stood still a moment. He made the sign of the cross.

Then he found his way to the door and fumbled until he found the keyhole and got the key into it. Then he turned it and pushed the door open—and the cat ran out into the passage before him.

FRANCES HODGSON BURNETT
The Lost Prince

Way down deep, we're all motivated by the same urges. Cats have the courage to live by them.

Jim Davis

Mabel the Stowaway

There is some truth in the assertion that the cat, with the exception of a few luxury breeds, such as Angora, Persians, and Siamese, is no domestic animal but a completely wild being. Maintaining its full independence, it has taken up its abode in the houses and outhouses of man, for the simple reason that there are more mice there than elsewhere.

Konrad Lorenz

Mabel smells travel coming on and of course she wants to be a member of the group. The fact that her master will be studying species of those delectable winged creatures adds to her excitement. Making sure not to be left behind in this frozen vulnerablelike state, she not only gets the attention she desires but also feels certain that our bird-loving ornithologist will find a spot for Mabel in whatever travel conveyance he chooses to employ. Happy trails, Mabel!

Handsome, precocious, determined, and at times, downright devilish. If only people could make of life what a cat finds everyday.

DOUGLAS EDWARDS

Unlike us, cats never outgrow their delight in cat capacities, nor do they settle finally for limitations. Cats, I think, live out their lives fulfilling their expectations.

IRVING TOWNSEND

Take a cat, nourish it well with milk,
And tender meat, make it a couch of silk,
But let it see a mouse along the wall,
And it abandons milk and meat and all,
And every other dainty in the house,
Such is the appetite to eat a mouse.

GEOFFREY CHAUCER

You become responsible

"There's nothing we can do now, except pray God to make Pat better," said Cecily.

I must candidly say that her tone savoured strongly of a last resort; but this was owing more to early training than to any lack of faith on Cecily's part. She knew and we knew, that prayer was a solemn rite, not to be lightly held, nor degraded to common uses. Felicity voiced this conviction when she said,

"I don't believe it would be right to pray about a cat."

"I'd like to know why not," retorted Cecily, "God made Paddy just as much as He made you, Felicity King, though perhaps He didn't go to so much trouble. And I'm sure He's abler to help him than Peg Bowen. Anyhow, I'm going to pray for Pat with all my might and main, and I'd like to see you try to stop me. Of course I won't mix it up with more important things. I'll just tack it on after I've finished asking the blessings, but before I say amen."

L. M. MONTGOMERY
The Story Girl

A cat can climb down from a tree without the assistance of the fire department or any other agency. The proof is that no one has ever seen a cat skeleton in a tree.

ANONYMOUS

forever for what you have tamed.

ANTOINE DE SAINT-EXUPERY

Maggie the Messmaker

Maggie came through the side door for this painting. That is, this cutie belongs to my son Matt's family, and after I paid the usual nominal cat-modeling fee, Maggie became the star. Seeing her here deep in quiet repose after her mischief-making party is actually not the same feline when awake. She is the most aggressive of all of the Wysocki family of cats and harbors an irascible spirit that surfaces often. So, even though in sleep she may appear to be the most joyous of felines, when awakened she can prove to be most interesting and a study in "cats-ophrenia." Maggie is a beautiful design in black and white and, I felt, the perfect personality to give this painting the character desired. Sleep deep, sweet mess-making beauty.

Max in the Adirondacks

All cats seem to have their favorite sleeping spot. For Max, it is the lure of the fishing shack, the anglers' paraphernalia, the fishy smells, the tobacco fumes, and the warmth of the radio and overhead lights that all make for a cozy day. Of course, after a few of these pleasant snoozes, he must commit to his obligation of another exciting *catsy* adventuresome column for the "Catskill Fibber." Max, being the laziest member of our brood, was my choice for this tranquil setting.

32

I welcome all creatures of the

Prowling his own quiet backyard or asleep by the fire, he is still only a whisker away from the wilds.

JEAN BURDEN

The door crept open with a disregarded whine as a pair of steel blue eyes fix upon two small plump feet dangling from the sitting room chair. Her tongue swept over the right patch of whiskers as if to say, "Tender toes, beware." Pressing her sleek gray body into the varnished wood floor, poised to pounce and take the fleshy prize, there could be only one master of this estate. And after all, it is a cat's condition to conquer and reign.

SIR CHARLES WALTHAM

world with grace.

HILDEGARD OF BINGEN

Once upon a time there lived a queen who had a beautiful cat, the colour of smoke, with china-blue eyes, which she was very fond of. The cat was constantly with her, and ran after her wherever she went, and even sat up proudly by her side when she drove out in her fine glass coach.

ANDREW LANG
Kisa the Cat

Thus encouraged, Daisy read her little paper, which was listened to with respectful attention.

"THE CAT"

"The cat is a sweet animal. I love them very much. They are clean and pretty, and catch rats and mice, and let you pet them, and are fond of you if you are kind. They are very wise, and can find their way anywhere. Little cats are called kittens, and are dear things. I have two, named Huz and Buz, and their mother is Topaz, because she has yellow eyes."

LOUISA MAY ALCOTT
Little Men

For he purrs in thankfulness, when God tells
him he's a good cat.
For he is an instrument for the children to
learn benevolence upon.

CHRISTOPHER SMART

Millie's Cat

There really isn't much to say about this primitive-styled version of my dimpled darling daughter's playfellow. The Early American oval rug has been the cat's mattress for years, as has the ball. It's simply a loveable portrait of Millie's Cat.

When I play with my cat, who
knows if I am not a pastime to her
more than she is to me?

MICHEL DE MONTAIGNE

I love my little kitty
Her coat is so warm.
And if I don't hurt her
She'll do me no harm
I won't pull her tail,
Or drive her away,
And kitty and I
Very gently will play.

CHILDREN'S NURSERY RHYME

Monty

Liz and I, while on a trip to Morro Bay, California, stopped in a turnout at Montana de Oro State Park to stretch and take a short walk in the woods. After only a few minutes, up came a little kitten that looked somewhat lost and forlorn. Right from the beginning we knew that he was no normal cat—almost all black (white spots on his chest and rear toes) and obviously malnourished from an early age. This was one smart cat though—he took about 30 seconds to worm his way into our hearts and into a one-way trip back home. Monty (besides occasionally assuming an out-of-this-world regal aura) is the house clown. He has a condition in which his coordination is off-kilter. Instead of walking like a normal cat, he moves his back legs like a kangaroo. He flips over, flops unexpectedly, and jumps higher and higher only to crash. As he runs full gallop headlong into a wall, we grit our teeth waiting for the dull thud. Monty's never-ending supply of nervous energy and gaucheness make for some entertaining times. It's a wonder he isn't loony—maybe he is! We could call him our recovering crash-a-holic because with so many painful contacts maybe he is finally beginning to realize his limitations. I don't think so, though. I believe that Monty is destined for limited stardom as our private loveable jester.

Four little Persians, but only one looked in my direction. I extended a tentative finger and two soft paws clung to it. There was a contented sound of purring, I suspect on both our parts.

GEORGE FREEDLEY

Bless their little pointed faces and their big, loyal, loving hearts. If a cat did not put a firm paw down now and then, how could his human remain possessed?

WINIFRED CARRIERE

© Charles Wysocki

© Charles Wysocki

It is as easy to hold quicksilver between your finger

"Meouw!" cried Snoop, as he came slowly out of the box in which he had ridden from Cuba.

Out walked the black cat. He looked about him strangely for a moment, and then began to purr, and rubbed up against Flossie's legs.

They all looked anxiously at Snap. The dog glanced at the cat, stretched lazily and wagged his tail. Snoop came over to him, and the two animals sniffed at each other, Mrs. Bobbsey holding Snap by the collar. Then, to the surprise of all, Snoop rubbed against the legs of the dog, and, on his part, Snap, wagging his tail in friendly, welcoming fashion, put out his red tongue and licked Snoop's fur.

"He's kissing Snoop! He's kissing Snoop!" cried Freddie.

LAURA LEE HOPE
The Bobbsey Twins at School

Rare creatures; smug at times, coy and aloof. Yet, with a curl of the tail or a nudge of their warm nose, their affection can enter as quickly as it goes.

LEWIS FAIRBANKS

What intenseness of desire
In her upward eye of fire!
With a tiger-leap half-way
Now she meets the coming prey...

WILLIAM WORDSWORTH

and thumb as to keep a cat who means to escape.

ANDREW LANG

A young grey cat that had been sleeping on the sofa jumped down and stretched, rising on its long legs, and arching its slim back. Then it sat considering for a moment, erect and kingly. And then, like a dart, it had shot out of the room, through the open window-doors, and into the garden.

D. H. LAWRENCE
Women In Love

Remington the Horticulturist

Remington was named for Frederic Remington, one of my favorite Western artists. When Remington came into our lives as a kitten via a friend and the local veterinarian's assistant, he immediately gave our hearts that "tug." He is the most tranquil of the family, loves to have his stomach scratched, and any lap in the house is his bed at any time. He is now eight years old—and, shall we say, a bit "chunky"—and seems to have a perpetual smile on his face, like maybe the garden is affording him extra pleasures.

The Cat. He walked by himself, and

Cats are rather delicate creatures, and they are subject to a good many ailments, but I never heard of one who suffered from insomnia.

JOSEPH W. KRUTCH

The smallest feline is a masterpiece.

LEONARDO DA VINCI

all places were alike to him.

RUDYARD KIPLING

Wild beasts he created later,
Lions with their paws so furious,
In the image of the lion
Made he kittens small and curious.

HEINRICH HEINE

Gentle eyes that see so much,
paws that have the quiet touch,
Purrs to signal "all is well"
and show more love than words could tell.
Graceful movements touched with pride,
a calming presence by our side
A friendship that takes time to grow
small wonder why we love them so.

AUTHOR UNKNOWN

When she
walked...she
stretched out long
and thin like a little
tiger, and held her
head high to look
over the grass as if
she were treading
the jungle.

SARAH ORNE JEWETT

> *Since each of us is blessed with only one life,*
> *why not live it with a cat?*
>
> ROBERT STEARNS

Too Pooped to Participate

You call to a dog and a dog will break its neck to get to you. Dogs just want to please. Call to a cat and its attitude is, "What's in it for me?"

LEWIS GRIZZARD

Our cat assumes this position from time to time on the rim of our loveseat in the den. I knew I would capture this pose on canvas someday. Knowing her love for climbing trees, I believe she made the perfect model for this work. Putting her outside, hanging on this limb, made a nice silhouette, with the testy mockingbirds upstairs ready to peck and irritate. It was a tempting location for a sleeping cat and proved to be great fun to compose and paint. I'm sure there are many people who have felt exactly as our cat did that day. She expresses an attitude that maybe we should purposely adopt now and then to slow down the day, and at the same time boost hammock sales!

© Charles Wysocki

It is perfectly possible (a fact which I have proved scores of times myself) to work not only with a cat in the room, but with a cat on one's shoulder or in one's lap. In a draughty room, indeed, the cat makes a superior kind of paperweight! Cats, to be sure, love to play on tables with loose papers and pens, but a little care will keep them from doing damage, and how welcome is the soft paw tap on the pen with the look of surprise that invariably follows, to the tired writer.

CARL VAN VECHTEN
THE TIGER IN THE HOUSE